50 CHRISTMASIEST BIBLE STORIES

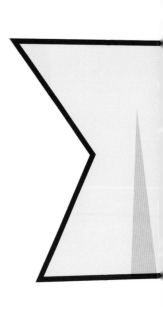

50 CHRISTMASIEST BIBLE STORIES

Andy Robb

CWR

Intro

Welcome to this very special, Christmassy edition of the *50 Bible Stories* series! If you're wondering how on earth I managed to find fifty stories in the Bible that are about Christmas then read on and all will be revealed.

What I *can* tell you now is that, from beginning to end, the Bible is all about Jesus in some way, shape or form and because Jesus is at the heart of Christmas, there's no shortage of Christmassy Bible stories.

If you've never picked up a Bible before let me quickly fill you in with some helpful info that's worth knowing …

FACT NUMBER ONE:

The Bible isn't actually just one book, but sixty-six books all rolled into one. Like a mini library. (In fact, the word 'Bible' actually means 'library'!)

FACT NUMBER TWO:

The Bible is divided into two parts. There's the Old Testament part, which covers everything from the beginning of the world up until just before Jesus was born. Then there's the New Testament part of the Bible, which kicks off around the time of Jesus' birth and covers all the things that happened after that.

FACT NUMBER THREE:

Everything that's in the Bible was God's idea.

Just like all of the other books in this series, each of the fifty Bible stories are retold with lots of fun and facts, a colourful cartoon and a bit at the end for you to look up in a real Bible.

If you're not sure how you go about reading a Bible (and I don't mean left to right, top to bottom) then here's what you need to know ...

Each book of the Bible has a name such as Genesis, Proverbs, Hebrews or Revelation. One Bible book that crops up quite a lot at Christmas is the book of Luke so we'll use this as an example. Most Bible books are broken up into chapters (though a handful only have one chapter), which are then divided into verses (like poems are).

So, if you wanted to check out the story of the shepherds from the Christmas story, you'd need to open a Bible to Bible book Luke, then turn the pages to find chapter 2 and verses 8 to 12. Here's how it's often written down:

LUKE 2:8-12

Take a look and see for yourself. Hope that was useful!

Right, that's me done. Time for you to dive into this fabulous feast of festive fun and facts (how's that for alliteration!) and enjoy the Christmasiest Bible stories I could find!

1
CHRISTMAS EVE
(AND ADAM)

There's a good chance that you're reading this book because you're a big fan of Christmas. Me too! Which is why I've decided to start things off with a nice Christmassy story from the Bible about a chap called Adam. I'm sure you've heard of him. He was the world's first person and lived a long, long time ago, thousands of years before the very first Christmas (when Jesus was born).

I guess right now you're thinking, 'Hang on a minute, what on earth has Adam got to do with Christmas if there was no Christmas way back then?' A good question. Here's your answer.

Adam and his wife Eve were best buddies with God, and all three of them loved spending time together. But that all came to an abrupt end when Adam and Eve disobeyed God – their wonderful friendship was ruined. For your information, it was none other than Satan (God's No. 1 enemy) who'd tempted Adam and Eve to do wrong. What a meanie.

Adam and Eve had been entrusted by God with taking care of the wonderful world that He'd created. Because of their wrongdoing it now gave Satan an open door to set up shop on the earth and to start making a mess of things.

The good news is that God still loved the world (and the people He'd created) and was determined to find a way to get things back to the way they'd once been. That's where Jesus (and Christmas) comes in. The Bible tells us something very interesting about Jesus that links Him with Adam. Just a heads-up: although this Bible bit doesn't actually mention Jesus by name, it's definitely about Him. (Read the whole chapter to find this out for yourself!)

Right, off you go to Bible book 1 Corinthians, chapter 15 and verse 45 to find that link.

A STAR IS BORN

Have you ever heard the phrase 'an overnight success'? It refers to someone like a pop star, or a sports star, who suddenly becomes famous. But here's the thing. Most people like this have actually been working away in the background for years and years and then, suddenly, all their hard work pays off and they make it to the big time, and everyone knows who they are.

Although, nowadays, most of us know about Jesus being born in Bethlehem, He wasn't always famous.

His birth never hit the headlines. Certainly, nobody had a clue who He was – apart from his mum and dad, a few relatives, a bunch of shepherds and some wise men.

So, thirty years later, when Jesus started healing sick people and teaching them about God, most people weren't that impressed. As far as they were concerned Jesus was just an ordinary carpenter's son from Nazareth.

If you had told them that Jesus was also the Son of God, they'd have probably laughed out loud or had you arrested for such an outrageous claim. And if you had told them that God (and not Jesus' human dad, Joseph) had made Jesus, they'd have thought you were stark raving bonkers.

But if they'd taken the time to read what some of their prophets had written about Jesus in the Old Testament part of the Bible, it would have put them straight.

Did you know that there's a bit in the Bible that was written yonks before Jesus was born (over 700 years in fact), which prepared the world for Jesus apparently appearing from nowhere?

A KING THING

One fella who pops up quite a lot in the Bible is Abraham. Not only did Abraham get the job of kick-starting the Israelite nation (who were known as God's chosen people), but he also got a thumbs-up from God for putting his trust in Him.

We catch up with Abraham just after he'd defeated some kings who'd kidnapped his nephew, who was called Lot, as well as Lot's family and all of Lot's worldly wealth. Which was a lot. Pardon the pun.

The king of Sodom (the place where Lot lived) was jolly grateful that all had ended well and went out to meet up with the man of the moment, Abraham.

As if one king wasn't enough, who should then show up but yet another king. This one was the king of Salem and he arrived armed with some bread and wine to help celebrate Abraham's victory. This king went by the name of Melchizedek (pronounced mel-kizzi-deck) and the Bible informs us that he was also a priest of God.

Without waiting to be asked, Melchizedek proceeded to speak a blessing from God over Abraham. How kind.

In return Abraham gave Melchizedek ten per cent of everything he had. Why on earth did he do that?

Sometimes in the Bible, things happen that are a pointer to something that will happen in the future. Abraham gave Melchizedek the gift because the king of Salem represented Jesus. A big clue regarding this was the bread and wine that Melchizedek brought. These two things would one day be very important in Jesus' life. Also, Melchizedek's name means 'king of righteousness', which gets a mention every year in most Christmas carol services.

HAVE YOU GOT ROOM FOR A FEW MORE KINGS?

See if you can find this in Bible book Isaiah, chapter 9 and verses 6 to 7.

TRUST TEST

You can't keep a good man down and we've got another Christmassy story featuring Abraham.

As I've already mentioned, Abraham was a man who trusted God wholeheartedly. Just when Abraham was probably thinking he couldn't trust God any more if he tried, something happened to test that trust.

God had told Abraham that he would have so many descendants that there would be no way he could ever count them. That's an awful lot of people! Unfortunately, there was a teensy weensy snag. Abraham and his wife (Sarah) couldn't have kids. Fortunately, God fixed that and (after a twenty-five-year wait) gave them a son called Isaac.

Just when everything seemed to be going well for him, God threw a spanner in the works and told Abraham to sacrifice (kill) Isaac to Him. Gulp! Seriously? Yep, seriously.

Once again Abraham obeyed God and travelled with Isaac to the mountain on which his son was to be killed (it was called Mount Moriah, just so you know). Although he couldn't quite work out how he would have any descendants if his only son was dead, Abraham figured that God could bring his son back to life if He wanted to.

Just when Abraham was about to kill his beloved Isaac, an angel stopped him in his tracks and said not to do it. God had no intention of having Isaac killed. He simply wanted to see how far Abraham was prepared to go in his trust of God. Seems like Abraham passed God's trust test with flying colours.

Does this all remind you of another story of sacrifice? Many years later, another beloved son, who was born in Bethlehem, was sacrificed for real.

Who are we talking about? Go to Bible book John, chapter 19 and verses 16 to 19.

JIGSAW JOE

I f you read the Bible from cover to cover (non-stop it should take you about three days), you'll soon discover that it all seems to fit together – a bit like a jigsaw puzzle.

Sometimes when you do a jigsaw you might wonder what that odd shaped bit in the middle has to do with the funny coloured corner piece. But when you step back and take a look at the finished thing, everything becomes clear. All the pieces come together to make one picture.

That's sort of what the Bible's like. You might, for example, wonder what the story of Joseph (not Jesus' dad but another Joseph) has to do with Jesus (and Christmas), but when you look at the big picture it soon becomes obvious.

In fact, this other Joseph is the very person I want to tell you about. Although Joseph's story in the Bible might look like it has absolutely zilch to do with this seasonal book, you're about to find out something that you may not have known.

First off, let me give you a quick rundown of Joseph's life. He was the favourite son of a guy called Jacob and for that reason his stepbrothers hated him. Joseph had a couple of dreams about ruling over them. And when he told them about this, they hated him even more. So his brothers sold him as a slave and he landed up in Egypt. God looked after Joseph even when he was thrown into prison for something he hadn't done. Years later, Joseph told the Egyptian king what his dreams meant and was rewarded by becoming Pharaoh's No 2. Joseph ended up saving the nation from famine by storing grain (for making bread).

Joseph is a bit of the Bible jigsaw who points the way to Jesus. Why? Because Jesus was also hated (and rejected). He was also loved greatly by His Father (God). And last but not least, He was a 'bread supplier'.

FOOD GLORIOUS FOOD

Right, hands up everyone who likes Christmas food ... Me too! Well most things. I'm not a big fan of nuts. Maybe that's because I'm nutty enough already!

Did you know that some of the scrummy things we eat at Christmas have something to do with the Bible and the story of Jesus?

For instance, mince pies. (Which reminds me: What do secret agents eat at Christmas? A mince spy! ... Just a little festive joke!) These popular little fruit pies weren't always

the way we know them. Once upon a time they were big and meaty. Eventually a fruit version was added with the addition of spices to reflect the gifts the wise men brought at Jesus' birth.

We've also got those wise men to thank for having a hand in Christmas cakes. Not literally of course. That wouldn't be hygienic! The Christmas cake recipe evolved and changed over hundreds of years into what we now enjoy, and became a firm Christmas favourite in the 1870s. These cakes had originally been eaten on what was called 'twelfth night' (6 January), which was twelve days after Christmas. (Hopefully you didn't need a calculator to work that one out.) This particular day (called Epiphany) was when Christians traditionally remembered the visit of the wise men to Jesus. Once again the spices in the Christmas cake represented the gifts of spice they brought to the young Jesus.

We've just got time to squeeze in one more Christmas food and that's the good old Christmas pud. A few quick facts. The pudding mixture was traditionally stirred from east to west in honour of, yes you guessed it, those wise men again (who came from the east). It was also often made with thirteen ingredients to represent thirteen particular people who appear in the Bible …

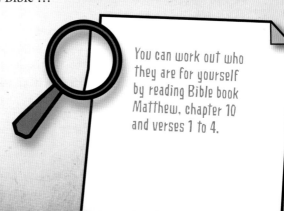

You can work out who they are for yourself by reading Bible book Matthew, chapter 10 and verses 1 to 4.

BAA HUMBUG!

One of the most famous people in the Bible was a chap called Moses.

One of his many claims to fame was rescuing the Israelite nation from slavery in Egypt. Okay, so he didn't do it single-handed. God sent a whole bunch of nasty plagues to convince the Egyptian pharaoh to let His special nation go. Unfortunately, Pharaoh was a rather stubborn ruler and was definitely in no mood to give up his free labour force any time soon.

The final punishing plague God planned to inflict upon the Egyptians was the death of every first-born creature. But God wanted to make sure that the angel He sent to carry this out didn't accidentally harm Moses' people, too. So the Israelites were instructed (by God) to kill a lamb and to paint its blood over the doorposts of their houses. When the angel arrived it would see the blood and pass over them.

Sorry, this isn't sounding very Christmassy at the moment but stick with me ...

The Israelites were also told to use the lamb meat to have a special meal (called Passover) to commemorate the day God rescued them.

Now let me tell you what this has to do with Christmas. Jesus was of course born as a baby. (That's the Christmas bit just to keep you happy.) Many years later, when He was a grown man, Jesus was killed (just like those Israelite lambs had been). The Bible says that because Jesus shed His blood, God is prepared to overlook (or pass over) all the bad things we've ever done.

Isn't it incredible that way back near the beginning of the Bible there's a big clue about Jesus and what He would one day do for us!

Now check out Bible book John, chapter 1 and verse 29 to find out someone who made the link between that story and Jesus.

We're staying with good old Moses for our next Christmassy Bible story.

Moses was a bit of a one-off when it comes to people in the Bible. Another of Moses' claims to fame was his amazing friendship with God. Moses spent loads of time chatting to God as if they were best buddies, which was quite unusual at the time.

Although there were other people in the Bible who knew God pretty well, you have to fast forward all the way to the New Testament part of the Bible to find someone who knew God as well as Moses. That person was, of course, none other than Jesus.

Moses and Jesus also had another thing in common. They were both prophets of God. Just in case you didn't know, a prophet is a person who tells people what God wants them to say. To do that they had to spend quality time with God, listening to Him and then passing on the info. And this is why our main man Moses gets the star treatment in this Christmas book. It's because the Bible said that God would raise up a prophet like Moses who would say the things God wanted them to say.

Yes, that person would turn out to be Jesus! So Moses (who lived around 1,500 years before the world's first Christmas) prepared the way for Jesus and gave people an idea of what to expect when He arrived, which was that He'd be a prophet of God.

You can find out that what I'm saying is true in Bible book Matthew, chapter 21 and verses 9 to 11.

9
SANTA BANTER

As you read this book, you'll discover that there's a lot about Christmas in the Bible, but one thing (or person) you won't find is Father Christmas or Santa Claus.

Having said that I thought I'd have a go at seeing if there was some way or other that I could link Santa Claus with the Bible. So here goes.

To do that we'll need to look at the history of our festive friend. Over the years, Santa has changed a lot from how we know him today. Things like his jolly white beard, living in the North Pole and flying through the air on a sleigh pulled by reindeer were all invented in America in the nineteenth century.

Santa Claus takes his name from a Dutch Christmas tradition and a chap called Sinterklaas, who filled wooden clogs with presents. And Sinterklaas actually comes from someone called Saint Nicholas (or Sint Nikolaas in Dutch).

Who's Saint Nicholas? I'll tell you.

He was a Turkish priest right back in the fourth century who was well known for his generosity to the poor. Saint Nick, so the story goes, didn't want people knowing that it was him who'd given the gifts, so he threw bags of gold into people's houses through the windows or chimneys. Some say the bags would land in the stockings or shoes that were left by the fireplace to dry. (It would explain that weird tradition we have of stockings and chimneys!) Now to the Bible bit.

Saints (like Nicholas was) actually pop up in the Bible. Sometimes people think that a saint is a top-notch Christian, but the Bible says that everyone who believes in Jesus is a saint.

CLUED UP

I f you turn on your TV, you'll not find it difficult to find a programme about detectives solving crimes. People seem to be fascinated with discovering what unusual clues will lead to.

The Old Testament part of the Bible is full of clues about Jesus being born and about the purpose of His life.

We're back with good old Moses because throughout the story of his life, God dropped in some important clues about Jesus that you could miss if you weren't concentrating. One of these less obvious clues has to do with water.

Many, many years after the shepherds and the wise men had come and gone, Jesus said something that seemed rather odd.

'Whoever believes in me ... rivers of living water will flow from within them.' (You can find this in the Bible book John, chapter 7 and verse 38.)

What on earth did that mean?

Jesus was actually talking about the Holy Spirit who would one day live in all of His followers. The Holy Spirit would refresh people just like water does.

This is where Moses comes in. Moses was leading the Israelites through a desert towards a wonderful new land that God had given them to live in.

As you can imagine, walking through a hot and dusty desert was thirsty work and very soon the Israelites began to grumble and moan that they were gasping for a drink.

Being the kind God that He is (and because there were no shops selling drinks nearby) God instructed Moses to go to a rock and command water to flow from it to refresh the people.

And that's why this is a Christmassy story, because it's a story with a clue that points to Jesus.

Did water really gush from that rock? See for yourself in Bible book Numbers, chapter 20 and verse 11.

CHRISTMAS COUNTDOWN

One of the best bits about Christmas is the big build-up to it. The Christmas season used to begin with Advent and the countdown to 25 December, but it now seems to start earlier each year. As soon as you're back to school after the summer break, the shops start to stock Christmas goodies. I remember being on holiday late one August and going into a shop to buy a postcard and they had a Christmas section in one corner! I have to confess that on a blisteringly hot day in the UK it looked very out of place.

But the Bible does the same thing and gives us the world's biggest build-up to Christmas. Almost from the start of the Bible, God begins to drop hints that He is going to send His one and only Son (Jesus) to earth to mend the broken friendship between us and Him. And then, after waiting thousands of years for Jesus to arrive, the Bible tells us that He only stayed around for thirty-three-ish years.

What's more, no sooner had Jesus begun to do the job for which God had sent Him (at the age of thirty) than He began to drop some hints of His own that He wouldn't be hanging around that much longer.

His disciples were bemused to say the least. What they didn't yet know was that when Jesus returned to heaven, He would send the Holy Spirit to keep them company and help them continue what He'd started.

We all know the Christmas story of how Jesus arrived as a baby, but how exactly was Jesus planning to make His exit from this world?

To find out, head to Bible book Acts, chapter 1 and verses 6 to 11.

12

DESERT DELIVERY

One of the best things about Christmas is all the lovely food you get to eat, such as turkey, Christmas pud, mince pies and of course, those tempting tree chocolates that you try to sneak when nobody's looking.

So this next Bible story qualifies to be in this book because it's all about food (of which there's lots of at Christmas). But there's also another reason, which you'll find out soon.

The Israelites, who star in this story, had recently escaped from Egypt and were slowly running out of food. Time for God to step in. Although the Israelites were getting grumpy about not having much to eat, God didn't take it personally. He told their leader Moses that food was on its way and that every morning they'd have a special delivery of food from Him.

Sure enough, the next morning the Israelites popped their heads outside their tents and, low and behold, the ground was covered with what looked like white corn flakes. Hmm, wonder what it tasted of? Yum, it was like wafers and honey.

The Bible tells us that it was actually called manna, which means 'What is it?' A question the Israelites were probably asking themselves.

The manna had a sell-by date on it. God said that the Israelites were to collect enough for one day at a time (and enough for two days on a Friday because Saturday was their special Jewish day off).

And now here's the other reason this has to do with Christmas. Just like the manna came from heaven to give life to the Israelites, so Jesus was sent from heaven (at Christmas) to give life to us.

Head to Bible book Exodus, chapter 16 and verse 13 to discover what food the Israelites had to eat in the evening.

13

FAKE SNAKE

What would you think if you looked inside your Christmas stocking on Christmas day to discover there was an Easter egg in it? You'd probably think it a bit odd, wouldn't you? But it's not as odd as you might think because Christmas and Easter are well and truly linked as far as the Bible is concerned.

Christmas, as we all know, is when Jesus came into the world as a baby. And Easter is all about how Jesus died on a wooden cross to take away sin (the bad things people do) from the world. Which means that there would have been no point in Christmas if Easter had never happened.

Right back in Moses' day something happened to the Israelites that would one day be repeated (in a similar way) by Jesus. Here's what happened. The Israelites were on their way to the land of Canaan, which God had given them as their home. Between you and me they were getting a bit fed up with the journey (and sometimes not having much to eat) and so they grumbled not only against their leader Moses, but also against God. This was a big mistake and God sent a load of venomous snakes to teach them a lesson. It did the trick and the Israelites realised the error of their ways and begged for God to get rid of the snakes. God told Moses to make a snake out of metal and put it up on a pole. Anyone who'd been bitten by a snake could look at it and live.

Now for the link to Jesus. When Jesus hung on a cross many years later (just like the snake was hung on a pole) anyone who looks to Him and accepts His sacrifice for them will be healed of their sin and will be able to live with God forever.

14
GONE GOAT

Did you know that there are a lot of phrases and expressions we use nowadays that originate in the Bible? Well there are and here are some examples: 'can a leopard change its spots?', 'a good Samaritan', 'in the twinkling of an eye' and 'scapegoat'.

Okay so that last one isn't actually a phrase, but it was a word first used in the Bible a long time ago, which we still use today to describe somebody who takes the blame for something.

You're probably wondering what has a goat got to do with Christmas aren't you? Reindeer, yes, but where do goats feature?

Well you're right that they don't crop up in the Christmas story about Jesus (although there could perhaps have been one in the stable at Bethlehem). And of course goats don't get a look in when it comes to all those Christmas traditions we love. But they do have something to do with Jesus and if you've been concentrating even a little bit as you've read this book, you'll know that Jesus has everything to do with Christmas.

In the Old Testament bit of the Bible you can read about how God allowed a goat to be sacrificed to take away the sin of the Israelites. The goat selected was sent into the wilderness as a sign that their sin had gone away. The goat that escaped was called the 'scapegoat'.

Just like that goat took the blame, Jesus took our blame and He took away all our sin.

Head to Bible book Job, chapter 19 and verse 20 to discover other everyday expressions that started in the Bible.

15
SAME NAME

I wonder if Jesus' human mum and dad (Mary and Joseph) had any idea what their little boy would grow up to be like? Of course they knew that He was special because He'd come from God, but what He would do with His life was anyone's guess. Except for God that is. God knew perfectly well the sort of things that lay in store for Jesus. Jesus' life on earth had been planned precisely.

In fact it had been so well planned that even well over a thousand years before Jesus was born, a guy called Joshua lived a life that dropped some big hints about Jesus.

For starters Jesus' name was simply another version of the name Joshua, which means 'God saves' (which is the reason Jesus came to our world in the first place – to rescue us).

Joshua was famous for leading the Israelite nation into what the Bible calls the 'promised land' or Canaan. It was a wonderful land, full of good things that God wanted the Israelites to enjoy.

Likewise Jesus would also make it possible for each and every one of us to enjoy all the good things that God has promised to those who are led by Him.

Joshua was a man of faith. That means he trusted God wholeheartedly. When he and some others went to spy on

Canaan, Joshua reported back to the Israelites that it was as good as God had said and that they should go and take the land just like God had told them to do.

While Jesus lived on earth He also trusted God completely.

And finally, Jesus spent a lot of His time alone with God. That was always a top priority for Him. Was it a top priority for Joshua, or was that where the comparisons stopped?

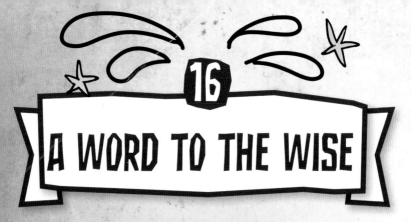

Although this book is all about Christmas and the Bible, did you know that the word 'Christmas' isn't actually mentioned in the Bible? Sorry to disappoint you young reader but that's just the way it is. Christmas is a made up word and is in fact two words joined together. Let me explain.

We'll start with the word Christ. At the time of Jesus' birth, a lot countries in the region where Jesus lived not only spoke their native language but also Greek. I haven't got time to explain why, just take it from me that's what they did.

The Greek word, Christ (or *christos*) was a translation of the Hebrew word, Messiah (or *mashiach*). Both of them meant one and the same thing, which was 'anointed' or 'the anointed one of God'. But because the New Testament part of the Bible was mostly written in Greek we've ended up using the word Christ. Still with me? Good!

To be anointed means to have God's Holy Spirit come upon you for a specific job. The Bible says that Jesus was (and is) God's anointed one and His job was to rescue us from living lives separated from God. So that's the Christ bit.

The 'mas' in Christmas is simply to do with a religious ceremony done by some churches, which is called a mass. Putting it all together, a Christ Mass would have been a yearly religious celebration of Jesus' birth. So now you know.

Just in case you feel a bit short-changed that I've not mentioned any Bible stories yet (and this is after all a Bible story book) allow me to resolve the matter.

Make tracks for Bible book John, chapter 1 and verses 35 to 41 and see if you can find the link to what I've been saying.

17
DAVE THE FAVE

I love Christmas carols and one of my favourites is *Once in Royal David's City*. The David in question was the same David who killed Goliath with a slingshot.

David was a shepherd boy who God handpicked to become the king of Israel. The Bible says that David was a man after God's own heart. In other words he loved to obey God and to do things God's way.

The city in the Christmas carol was Bethlehem, the place where David grew up. Because of David's love for God, God promised that not only would his royal family go on forever, but that God's Messiah (Jesus) would one day be born into it. Wow, that's some promise!

Sure enough, that's precisely what happened, and Jesus was born in Bethlehem too.

As you will have discovered (if you read this book from cover to cover) Jesus was lots of different things. Not only was He a Saviour but He was also a King.

Jesus was born into our world at Christmas to bring God's kingdom from heaven to earth. To have a kingdom you've got to have a king – and that King was Jesus.

God's kingdom is anywhere that people allow Jesus to be No. 1 in their lives. Having Jesus as our King means that He rules over our lives to take care of us and to protect us.

So it was no coincidence that Jesus was born into King David's royal family line.

AMAZING ANCESTORS

Family trees have become really popular over the past few years and lots of people want to find out who their ancestors were and what they were like.

Although Jesus was God, He was also a human being, so the Bible traces Jesus' family history through His human dad Joseph's side. We have Bible books Matthew and Luke to thank for telling us about all the people who led up to Jesus being born at Christmas. We've not got room to give everyone a mention here, but here's a few of them starting with the world's very first man, Adam. Actually that's cheating because Adam is everybody's ancestor.

How about Noah? You've probably heard of him. He was the chap who built a humongous boat (the ark) to rescue his family and at least a couple of every animal from a fearsome flood that covered the world.

Next up we've got Abraham. He gets the credit for starting the Jewish nation, into which Jesus was born. Nice one Abraham!

One of Jesus' more unusual ancestors was a lady called Rahab who swapped sides and helped the Israelites conquer the walled city of Jericho, in which she lived.

Then there's Ruth. She was another distant relative of Jesus who set her heart on following God and ended up having a whole Bible book named after her. How cool is that!

And finally King David also pops up in Jesus' family tree. He was a man who tried to live his life to please God as ruler of Israel.

Each of these people (and those I've not named) played a part in getting things ready for the arrival of their descendant Jesus at Christmas.

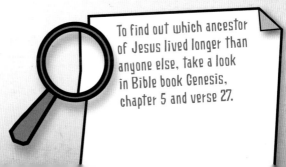

To find out which ancestor of Jesus lived longer than anyone else, take a look in Bible book Genesis, chapter 5 and verse 27.

SIBLING QUIBBLING

We're keeping on the family theme for this next bit.

Did you know that Jesus had brothers and sisters? The Bible even gives us their names if you're interested. James, Joseph, Simon and Judas. No names for his sisters though. By the sounds of it there were a few of them.

How amazing it must have been for Jesus' mum and dad to know that their first child was God's Son, but I wonder if they treated Him any different from their other kids?

That's something the Bible doesn't tell us. It also doesn't tell us if Jesus' siblings knew anything about Him being born with the animals and how shepherds and wise men came to worship their big brother.

What the Bible does tell us is that when Jesus was a man and had started teaching in public about God and healing people, His brothers and sisters thought He'd lost the plot and tried to persuade Him to stop.

Much to everyone's surprise, Jesus told the crowds listening that His family was anybody who did the will of God. A bit odd don't you think?

Nope!

The whole point of Jesus coming to earth (at Christmas) was to get as many people into God's family as possible. Jesus wasn't saying that our human families aren't important. It's just that our top priority is getting into God's family so that we can then love our human families even more.

As for Jesus' family, the Bible tells us that James and Jude eventually came round to believing that Jesus was the Son of God. Who knows, maybe the others did also.

Did you know that you can join God's family if you want to?

ZIP THE LIP

Shortly before Jesus was born, a man named Zechariah had a surprise visit.

Zechariah was a priest who served in the temple of Israel's capital city, Jerusalem. He was going about his duties one particular day when who should rock up but an angel of God, no less.

Angels have plenty to do and don't usually drop by just for no reason. Zechariah was gobsmacked. What was this all about?

While Zechariah stood there, probably open-mouthed with surprise, the angel filled him in with why he was there.

Up to that point Zechariah and his wife Elizabeth (a relative of Jesus' mum, Mary) had no kids. Not because they didn't want them, but because they couldn't. That was about to change.

The angel (Gabriel) gave Zechariah the good news that God was going to give them a boy who they were to call John. God had a special job for John. When he grew up he'd set the scene for the arrival of Jesus. Okay, so the angel didn't say this in so many words but if you read about John later in the Bible, you'll find out that John was indeed preparing the way for Jesus.

Then Zechariah made a bit of a blunder. Rather than just taking the angel at his word he questioned how he would know that this was all for real. Oh dear. Silly Zechariah.

If Zechariah had been lost for words before, he was certainly going to be from now on. Because he hadn't believed the angel, Zechariah found he could not speak at all after Gabriel had left!

21
SCARY FOR MARY

I f you've read the story before this one, you'll have already been introduced to the angel Gabriel. Christmas is a busy time for most people and this first Christmas was no exception for Gabriel. He had lots to do in getting everything ready for Jesus being born.

Gabriel's next visit was to a young lady called Mary. Mary lived in a place called Nazareth and was engaged to a chap called Joseph.

There's probably no easy way for an awesome angel of God to introduce himself, so when Gabriel appeared to Mary it's no surprise that the Bible said she was greatly troubled.

Mary was also a little taken aback by the angel's opening lines: 'Greetings, you who are highly favoured! The Lord is with you.'

What had she done to deserve this?

While Mary was still trying to get her head round what was happening, Gabriel attempted to calm her down and to break some good news to her. Well, hopefully Mary would think it was good news.

'Do not be afraid, Mary, you have found favour with God. You will conceive and give birth to a son, and you are to call him Jesus. He will be great and will be called the Son of the Most High. The Lord God will give him the throne of his father David, and he will reign over Jacob's descendants for ever; his kingdom will never end.' (You can find this in Bible book Luke, chapter 1 and verses 28 to 33.)

All that Mary could think to ask was how this could be – after all she wasn't married yet.

WOAH, JOE!

I sometimes feel a little bit sorry for Jesus' human dad, Joseph. He was engaged to be married to Mary but before they could tie the knot he discovered she was pregnant and the baby wasn't his. What was he to do?

There would be a scandal when word got out that Mary was going to be an unmarried mum.

It appears that Joseph was a decent sort of chap and didn't want to shame Mary publicly. The Bible says that he planned to quietly break off the engagement without a fuss.

God had other plans.

Who knows whether Mary had told Joseph that the child she was carrying had been put there by God, but if so, Joseph obviously wasn't buying it. Which is why Joseph had his very own personal visit from an angel. It could well have been Gabriel again. Who knows. The Bible doesn't let on.

Joseph's angel visit wasn't like Mary's. The angel spoke to Joseph in a dream. Here's what the angel said in Bible book Matthew, chapter 1 and verses 20 and 21: 'Joseph son of David, do not be afraid to take Mary home as your wife, because what is conceived in her is from the Holy Spirit.

She will give birth to a son, and you are to give him the name Jesus, because he will save his people from their sins.'

Did Joseph still go ahead with breaking off his engagement to Mary or did he believe what the angel had said?

Your answer is found in Bible book Matthew, chapter 1 and verses 24 to 25.

Have you ever noticed how some Christmas cards picture Jesus with a little glowing halo around His head? Of course there's a very good reason for that, which is to show us that He was not just any ordinary baby, but God.

But although Jesus was (and is) God, He was also very much a human being.

I know it's not very good maths but the best way I can describe it was that He was one hundred per cent human and also one hundred per cent God.

The God part of Jesus was what helped Jesus live a perfect life in His body.

Having said that, Jesus was still very much a human baby, so I doubt if He ever had a holy glow around His head to make Him stick out from all the other babies in Nazareth.

So songs like *Away in a manger*, where we sing, 'The cattle are lowing, the baby awakes, but little Lord Jesus, no crying He makes', are probably taking things a bit too far. If Jesus had a human body like the rest of us, then He certainly felt pain and shed a tear or two.

But it was the God part of Jesus that kept Him on the straight and narrow. My guess is that even as a baby, Jesus was aware of Father God in heaven who would help Him do this.

Years later, Jesus was still relying on His heavenly Father to finish the job for which He'd sent Him to earth.

24
BOUNCING BABY

I don't know about you but when I get some good news I want to share it.

Mary (Jesus' mum) had just been told by an angel that she'd been handpicked by God to give birth to God's Son and it would be the Holy Spirit, not Jesus' dad Joseph, who would bring this about.

In the history of the world, nothing like this had ever happened before (or since). Mary must have been bowled over when the angel had told her what was going to happen. Imagine giving birth to a child who was God's Son! Mind-blowing or what!

It's pretty obvious that Mary couldn't contain her excitement because the Bible tells us that she hot-footed it from her home town of Nazareth to the foothills of a Judea, to break the news to her relative Elizabeth.

This was no mean feat. The journey could have taken her well over a week. But there was just no stopping Mary. She was so excited!

My guess is that there was another reason Mary wanted to make this trek. The angel had also informed Mary that Elizabeth (who was quite old) was going to have a baby as

well, and that she was already six months pregnant. I'll bet Mary was busting to find out if this was true and to see what God was up to.

As Mary announced her arrival, the baby inside Elizabeth leapt in her tummy. Her baby (John) obviously knew that Mary's baby was no ordinary boy. That wasn't all. The Bible says that Elizabeth was immediately filled with the Holy Spirit.

Elizabeth was chuffed that she'd had a personal visit from Jesus (even though He was still in His mummy's tummy).

Mary was overjoyed as well and launched forth into a song, which summed up her feelings.

Mary's song is not available to download but you can find it in Bible book Luke, chapter 1 and verses 46 to 55.

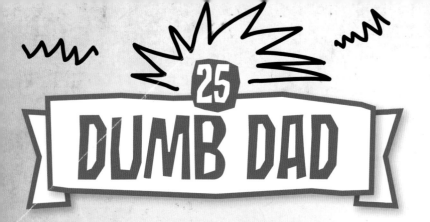

25
DUMB DAD

This next Christmassy Bible story follows on from the last one.

A few stories back I mentioned a chap called Zechariah who couldn't quite get his head around the fact that God was going to enable him and his wife (Elizabeth) to have their first child. It didn't help that they were both old and had never been able to have kids up until then.

Because Zechariah had questioned the angel who broke the news to him as to how this could be possible, he was struck dumb.

Elizabeth and Zechariah's neighbours weren't quite so doubting and were over the moon when they were told the good news. What they couldn't understand was why Zechariah and Elizabeth were going to call their son John. All would soon be revealed!

Eight days after the birth, when the time came to name their baby boy, Zechariah was asked what the child's name would be. Everyone assumed that he'd be called Zechariah, in keeping with family tradition, but not so.

Zechariah still couldn't speak so he got a writing tablet and wrote down the name 'John'. That was a bit of a surprise. Nobody in the family had been called that before. But Zechariah had learned his lesson and was now prepared to take God at His word. John was the name the angel said to give the boy, so John it was. End of story.

And with that Zechariah's speech was restored.

Just in time for Zechariah to follow in Mary's footsteps and to let rip with some poetic words of his own.

BIRTHDAY BOY

You'd think that after the big build up in the Bible to the birth of Jesus (I seem to have put a lot of 'b's in this sentence!) there'd maybe at least be a few chunky chapters milking the moment and giving us loads of detail about what actually happened. Nope.

Jesus' birth only pops up in just two Bible books. In Bible book Luke, there are just six verses about this extraordinary event and in Bible book Matthew all you get is a heads-up that the thing has happened. That's your lot! If you're a fast reader there's a good chance you could even skip right over it.

Anyway, for the record, Jesus was born in a place called Bethlehem, which was about a seventy mile trek for His mum and dad (Mary and Joseph) from their hometown of Nazareth, in Israel.

The reason they'd had to make the trip was because the Roman ruler of the region (Caesar Augustus) had decided to do a head count of everyone he ruled over. All the people had to register at the place in which they'd been born (or at least where the men had).

Because of the count up (or census), Bethlehem was chock-a-block with visitors and Mary and Joseph struggled to find somewhere to stay. They ended up having to kip down with the animals at someone's house, which to be honest was not exactly ideal.

And so that's where Jesus (God's Son) was born and with it the world had its very first Christmas day.

To find out the rather unusual place Mary and Joseph found for their baby boy to sleep in, go to Bible book Luke, chapter 2 and verse 7.

27
FLOCK SHOCK

Nothing that happens in the Bible is by accident. God has made sure everything that's written down is precisely what He wants us to know.

When I tell you that our next Christmassy Bible story stars a bunch of lowly shepherds, you won't be surprised if I tell you that this was for a very good reason – which I'll let on in a bit.

It might have been just an ordinary night for those shepherds, watching over their flocks on the hills surrounding Bethlehem. Not for long.

Bam!

From out of nowhere an angel appeared and proceeded to fill them in with the astounding news that Jesus, the Saviour of the world, had just been born nearby. Being a helpful angel, he also gave them a clue or two as to how they could find Jesus (if they so wished).

Before the shepherds had a chance to work out what to do next, the whole sky was buzzing with angels praising God for Jesus' birth.

So here's why those lowly shepherds get a look in.

Remember the stuff earlier on in this book about lambs being sacrificed? You do? Glad you were paying attention.

Well later on in the story of Jesus' life, we're going to discover that He gets called the Lamb of God because He makes a whopper of a sacrifice for us (the greatest sacrifice of all).

But that's not all. The Bible also calls Jesus 'the Good Shepherd' because of the way He cares for us.

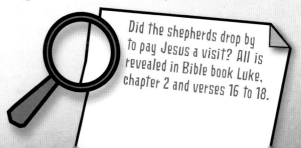

Did the shepherds drop by to pay Jesus a visit? All is revealed in Bible book Luke, chapter 2 and verses 16 to 18.

28
WISE GUYS

Now listen carefully. I'm about to say something that might just spoil your Christmas, but I don't want you to blame me. It's in the Bible so I'm completely in the clear.

You know how the wise men (or magi) show up in Christmas nativity plays and hand over the gifts of gold, frankincense and myrrh to baby Jesus? Well, how can I put it? That's not actually quite how things happened.

Before you start sobbing your heart out because I've ruined your Christmas, you need to know that Jesus did have a visit from some wise men from a distant land. It's just that they didn't rock up at the same time as the shepherds I told you about in the previous story.

By the time these visitors from the east showed up (helpfully guided there by a star), baby Jesus could well have been more like toddler Jesus.

How do I know that?

Well I don't for certain but what I do know is that when these so-called wise men turned up in Jerusalem to ask King Herod if he had any idea where this new king of the Jews had been born, Herod wasn't a happy bunny.

No way was a kid going to have his crown or, for that matter, his throne. There was only room for one king in the land and he was it.

The wise men did in fact find Jesus (and deliver their gifts) but Herod wasn't quite so friendly. He ordered every child (under the age of two) in the region in which he thought Jesus was living, to be killed. Which is why I'm inclined to think Jesus might have been approaching the age of two the time the wise men visited.

How did Jesus escape from horrid Herod? Check out Bible book Matthew, chapter 2 and verses 13 to 14.

29

PECULIAR PREZZIES

We're going to stick with the wise men from the Christmas story so that we can find out a little more about them.

Before I go any further I'm going to need to put the record straight and tell you that nowhere in the Bible does it say that there were actually three of these visitors from a distant land in the east. What it does say is that there were three gifts – which we're going to talk about in a moment.

These exotic visitors also tend to get called the three kings, or magi (priests who had a particular interest in stars). Over time they were even given the names of Balthasar, Caspar, Melchior.

What's amazing is how they found about Jesus in the first place. Here's what they said to King Herod when they finally arrived in Israel.

'Where is He who has been born King of the Jews? For we saw His star when it rose and have come to worship him.'

How on earth did they work out all that from a star? Your guess is as good as mine. And when they'd said cheerio to Herod, the star was ready and waiting to guide them the last leg of the journey to where Jesus was living. Amazing!

What's even more astounding though is the gifts that they brought to young Jesus. Gold, frankincense and myrrh. Not a toy train set or box of building blocks in sight.

Gold represented the fact that Jesus had been born King of the Jews.

Frankincense represented the fact that one day Jesus would be what the Bible calls our High Priest. He'd be the middle-man in heaven between us and God.

And finally myrrh (pronounced merr) represented the afflictions that Jesus would one day have to suffer.

WHAT A STAR YOU ARE

To find out what happened when they delivered their prezzies to Jesus, go to Bible book Matthew, chapter 2 and verses 11 and 12.

30

TEMPLE TWOSOME

If you've read the previous stories in this festive book, you'll be well aware that not many people at the time of Jesus' birth had the foggiest idea that God's one and only Son was in the neighbourhood.

We know of course that the shepherds had an angel to break the news and the wise men had a star to signpost them to Jesus, but there were a couple more people who also got in on the act as well. Let me tell you about them.

Jewish parents (like Jesus' mum and dad) were required to take their babies (when they were just eight days old) to the Temple to dedicate them and their life to God. It was their way of saying 'Thank You' to God for giving them their child.

As part of this ceremony, Mary and Joseph had to give a sacrifice of two pigeons.

While this was all happening, a guy called Simeon was also at the Temple and he was now making a beeline for them. The Bible says that Simeon took God seriously. In return God had shown him that, before he popped his clogs (died), he would get to clap eyes on the person God had handpicked to rescue the Jewish people (and, for that matter, everyone else in the world as well). God led Simeon to the temple courts and there he waited for something special to happen. Right on cue, Jesus appeared (along with his mum and dad of course). Simeon took Jesus in his arms and thanked God that he had finally seen God's Messiah. (Messiah is the name Jewish people gave to the person God would send to rescue them). God then inspired Simeon to predict that Jesus would grow up to be a man who changed the world.

WISH I COULD BE SO UPBEAT ABOUT ALL THIS!

If you want to find out who else had something to say about Jesus at the Temple, head to Bible book Luke, chapter 2 and verses 36 to 38.

31

MERRY WORD-MAS

ight, are you ready to have your brain stretched? Not literally of course. That would look a bit odd and probably make your ears stick out a lot.

What I mean is, are you up for getting your head round a Bible story that has everything to do with Christmas but doesn't usually get as much of a look-in as some of the other more Christmassy Christmas stories, such as the shepherds and then wise men?

You are? Good!

We're heading to Bible book John and the very first chapter and first four verses where it says this: 'In the beginning was the Word, and the Word was with God, and the Word was God. He was with God in the beginning. Through him all things were made; without him nothing was made that has been made. In him was life, and that life was the light of all mankind.'

Although it doesn't say so in as many words, this Bible bit is talking about Jesus. If you keep reading the Bible passage it soon becomes clear.

Anyway, in a nutshell, John is telling us that Jesus was and is God. He also informs us that Jesus was alive and kicking when the world began and, more to the point, Jesus was involved in the creation of the world. Last, but not least, everything gets its life from Jesus. That means you, me, the plants and flowers. The whole universe in fact.

Skipping ahead a few verses to number 14, John then drops in the Christmassy bit: 'The Word became flesh and made his dwelling among us.'

YOU'RE RIGHT, THAT DID STRETCH MY BRAIN

Want to know what that looked like? Head to Bible book Luke, chapter 2 and verses 11 and 12.

32

ANGEL OVERLOAD

Seeing that this book is all about Christmas, it wouldn't be right if we didn't mention a few Christmas carols along the way. Although you won't find carols mentioned anywhere in the Bible, many of them are based on Bible stories.

The idea of singing songs about Christmas was actually nicked from pagans (people who worshipped nature or other gods, rather than the one true God), whose carols were a mixture of singing and dancing. The Christians, way back then, copied the idea and began writing carols about Jesus and Christmas. Quite a few of these carols are about angels. That's because angels pop up all over the place in the Christmas story.

For instance, an angel rocked up to tell Mary that she was going to give birth to Jesus. An angel informed Jesus' dad that his fiancé, Mary, was pregnant and a whole sky-full of angels announced the news of Jesus to some shepherds.

So as you can see, Christmas was a busy time for angels.

Here are a few of my favourite Christmas carols that feature angels.

First up we've got *Angels from the Realms of Glory*. This carol cunningly covers just about the whole Christmas story. Nice one!

Hark! The Herald Angels Sing reminds everyone that Jesus was actually going to be King.

And *While Shepherds Watched Their Flocks* retells the story of when the angels turned up, unannounced, to a bunch of shepherds in Bethlehem.

I'll let you in on a little secret. When I was about your age we used to change the words when we sang this carol.

Instead of singing 'While shepherds watched their flocks by night', we used to sing 'While shepherds washed their socks by night'. Naughty I know, but we found it funny.

Did you know that those angels also did a bit of carol singing of their own (well sort of)?

We're going to stick with the subject of Christmas carols for just a little longer. Not only are they fun to sing but they're also a great way of hearing the story of Jesus' birth.

One popular carol that does that is *The Holly and the Ivy.* I'll bet you've sung it, haven't you?

Although Christians have made this carol their own, it was probably originally a pagan song with a different meaning. But the version that gets sung at Christmas is very much about Jesus. I'll explain.

When we sing 'The holly bears a blossom as white as lily flower, and Mary bore sweet Jesus Christ to be our sweet Saviour', it's about Jesus' purity (like a white blossom).

The next bit, 'The holly bears a berry as red as any blood, and Mary bore sweet Jesus Christ to do poor sinners good', is about Jesus' blood that would one day flow from His body as He gave His life for you and me.

'The holly bears a prickle as sharp as any thorn, and Mary bore sweet Jesus Christ on Christmas Day in the morn.' That's all to do with the crown of thorns that would be placed on Jesus before He was killed.

And finally, 'The holly bears a bark as bitter as any gall, and Mary bore sweet Jesus Christ for to redeem us all'. You can do your own detective work for this one to find out what it refers to in the Bible.

So you'll need to go to Bible book Matthew, chapter 27 and verses 32 to 34.

NO SNOW

Now it wouldn't be Christmas if there wasn't any mention of snow, so I've been having a rummage around in the Bible to see if I could find anything to do with that white, fluffy stuff.

One place you're not going to find snow is in the story of Jesus. Yes they do sometimes have snow in Israel (where Jesus was born) but if it fell at the time of Jesus' birth nobody has said anything.

Snow, or the word snow, does crop up here and there in the Bible.

Moses' sister, Miriam's skin turned as white as snow with leprosy because she sinned against God.

According to Bible book Psalms (pronounced 'sarms'), chapter 148 and verse 8, lightning, hail, snow, clouds, and stormy winds all do what God tells them.

And the Bible also says that one day Jesus will return to earth in all His heavenly splendour and His appearance will be like lightning, and His clothes as white as snow.

But my challenge was to find a Bible bit about snow that has something to do with Jesus or Christmas. Here's what I found.

In Bible book Psalms, chapter 51 and verse 7 it says: 'Cleanse me with hyssop, and I shall be clean; wash me, and I shall be whiter than snow.'

Just so you know, hyssop was a herb that people used a lot in Bible times, which has loads of uses, including cleaning things.

In this Bible bit, it's not really talking about giving someone a wash and a scrub from head to toe, but making them clean inside so that they become a better person.

The Bible tells us that Jesus died to give us a new start in life and to make us good inside, like God is. It's no coincidence then that hyssop shows up again at the time of Jesus' death to underline what I've just said.

LOOKS LIKE I'LL JUST HAVE TO DO MY SNOW ANGEL WITHOUT THE SNOW

Find what I'm talking about in Bible book John, chapter 19 and verses 29 to 30.

TWENTY-FIFTH MYTH

I t may not come as a big surprise if I tell you that there hasn't always been Christmas. Thought so. You'd probably worked out that it only started when Jesus was born. But did you know that the date on which we celebrate Christmas has got absolutely nothing to do with the date of Jesus' birth?

As a matter of fact, people didn't start celebrating Christmas until around the fourth century (that's roughly sixteen hundred years ago) and when they did, it was for a particular reason – which I'll explain.

Way back then (and especially if you happened to live in the Roman empire), you'd have enjoyed nothing more on 25 December than a good old knees-up in honour of the sun god, Mithras.

The Christians thereabouts weren't too keen on the idea of making a big thing of Mithras and had a bit of a brainwave. Why not gatecrash the Mithras celebrations and use the same date to celebrate Jesus' birthday instead. Genius! So that's what they did.

Now if you're wondering when Jesus was actually born (it wasn't 25 December), I may be able to help you out.

A lot of people have come to the conclusion that it could have been some time in September and here's why.

The shepherds who came to visit baby Jesus had been sleeping out under the stars. You'd not do that in December in Israel.

Someone has worked out that John (Elizabeth and Zechariah's boy) was born in March and John was six months older than Jesus.

Lastly, Jesus' mum and dad travelled to Bethlehem shortly before His birth because of a Roman census. A census in winter would have made it too difficult for people to travel.

To discover who was responsible for that census, head for Bible book Luke, chapter 2 and verses 1 to 6.

36
HOLY HEADS-UP

Did you know that there are adverts in the Bible? You didn't? Well there are.

In fact there are hundreds and hundreds of them if you must know!

You could be forgiven for missing them because they're not adverts for things like nose hair clippers or cat food but are actually adverts for events that were going to happen some time in the future.

And the Bible doesn't call them adverts but prophecies.

Prophecies are information God shares with people (who are called prophets) well in advance so that everyone gets a bit of a heads-up that something is going to happen.

The Old Testament part of the Bible has around 350 of these prophecies, which specifically advertised to the Jewish nation that Jesus was on His way and also loads of stuff about the sort of life He would live.

These adverts (as I like to call them) were dictated by God to a number of different people, hundreds of years before Jesus was born. What's amazing is that when you read the New Testament part of the Bible, you can check out to see how they were fulfilled.

Why did God give the world advance warning that His one and only Son was on His way to the earth? Simple. So when Jesus arrived, people knew that He was the Messiah sent by God who they'd been waiting for.

Here's a Christmassy advert for Jesus that appears in Bible book Micah, chapter 5 and verse 2: 'But you, Bethlehem Ephrathah, though you are small among the clans of Judah, out of you will come for me one who will be ruler over Israel, whose origins are from of old, from ancient times.'

To see how this prophecy was fulfilled, check out Bible book Matthew, chapter 2 and verses 1 to 6.

PROLIFIC PROPHET

Time for some more adverts (or prophecies) about Jesus and Christmas.

There's one particular Bible advert that would have not only sounded a bit unusual to people at the time but would have seemed downright impossible.

The prophet who delivered this advert was none other than a guy called Isaiah (pronounced eye-si-er). Isaiah was a bit of a big shot prophet in the Old Testament, so much so that he has a whole Bible book named after him, which you'll not be surprised to discover is called Isaiah.

Isaiah was a prolific prophet, meaning he had a lot of prophecies, including a few about Jesus.

One of his astounding adverts about Jesus can be found in Bible book Isaiah, chapter 7 and verse 14. Here's how it went: 'Therefore the Lord himself will give you a sign: the virgin will conceive and give birth to a son, and will call him Immanuel.'

The virgin in question was Jesus' mum, Mary.

If you've been reading through this book without jumping ahead (and if you have, tut tut!) then you'll know that Jesus' mum was given her baby boy by God and not by her husband Joseph.

Here's a fascinating fact. Isaiah would have had to live another 730 or so years if he'd wanted to see his advert about Jesus come to pass. He didn't!

Want to look up the Bible bit that tells you how Isaiah's prophecy came true?

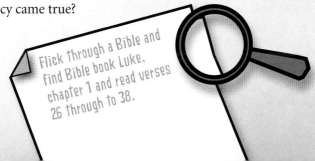

Flick through a Bible and find Bible book Luke, chapter 1 and read verses 26 through to 38.

Most people know about the wise men coming to visit Jesus at Christmas.

Before they dropped in on Jesus (with their gifts of gold, frankincense and myrrh), these mysterious visitors from the east popped in to say 'Hi' to Israel's King Herod and to ask for directions to where this new-born King of the Jews (Jesus) was.

Herod didn't actually know where Jesus was born but his religious leaders knew that there was a prophecy that pinpointed the precise location of Jesus' birth. It was the one about Bethlehem that I flagged up earlier.

Now back to the king bit.

Good old Isaiah had pipped the wise men to the post with that bit of info hundreds of years earlier by announcing in Bible book Isaiah, chapter 9 and verses 6 and 7 that Jesus was going to be King. This is how Isaiah's advert for Jesus went: 'For to us a child is born, to us a son is given, and the government will be on his shoulders. And he will be called Wonderful Counsellor, Mighty God, Everlasting Father, Prince of Peace. Of the greatness of his government and peace there will be no end. He will reign on David's throne and over his kingdom, establishing and upholding it with justice and righteousness from that time on and for ever.'

Horrid Herod was in no mood to put out the welcome mat for another king in his land, he wanted Jesus dead.

The good news is that God sent an angel to warn Jesus' dad about the king's dastardly plan and to flee to Egypt with his wife and son.

TELLING TALES

I have a confession to make.

I'm guilty of referring to the account of Jesus' birth in the Bible as 'The Christmas Story'. I'll probably do it a few more times in this book but there is a danger that using the word 'story' makes it sound a bit like fiction or a fairy tale, which is far from the truth.

Did you know that there is oodles and oodles of historical evidence to prove that Jesus was as real as you and I? Yep, there is. But not everything you'll find in the Bible is for real. Jesus told lots of stories, which He simply made up. The reason Jesus told these stories (called parables) was to teach people about God. All in all there were over forty of them.

What's amazing is that long before Jesus was ever a baby in a manger or there were shepherds watching over their flocks by night, the Bible slipped out a couple of prophecies advertising these parables.

In Bible book Psalms, chapter 78 and verse 2 it says this about Jesus: 'I will open my mouth with a parable'. Check it out for yourself.

Then our good friend, Isaiah, said this in Bible book Isaiah (obviously), chapter 6 and verse 9: 'Be ever hearing, but never understanding; be ever seeing, but never perceiving.'

Why on earth would Jesus want to tell stories or parables that people wouldn't understand or miss the point? I'll tell you.

Jesus wasn't trying to be difficult, it was just that His stories contained stuff about God that you could only understand if you chose to believe that He was the Son of God.

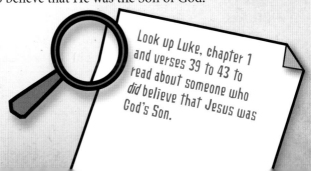

Look up Luke, chapter 1 and verses 39 to 43 to read about someone who *did* believe that Jesus was God's Son.

40

MERRY EASTER

I think we've got room to squeeze in one more look at some adverts from the Bible, which announced that Jesus was on His way.

Because everything in the Bible has some sort of link to Jesus and because Jesus has everything to do with Christmas, we could probably make a Christmassy link with just about every story in the Bible. But that might be pushing it a bit too far.

One part of the Bible that you *can* connect with the Christmas story is Easter. That's because the whole point of Jesus being born (at Christmas) was to eventually give His life for us on a cross (at Easter).

So we're going to make tracks for Bible book Psalms, chapter 41 and verse 9 where it tells us this about Jesus last days on earth: 'Even my close friend, someone I trusted, one who shared my bread, has turned against me.' You can read how this was fulfilled in Bible book Matthew, chapter 26 and verse 23.

A few of the prophets actually revealed some of the things that would happen when Jesus was crucified, which included being spat upon and hit.

'I offered my back to those who beat me, my cheeks to those who pulled out my beard; I did not hide my face from mocking and spitting.' That's from our friend Isaiah, chapter 50 and verse 6.

Finally in Psalms, chapter 22 and verse 18 there's this prophecy about Jesus: 'They divide my clothes among them and cast lots for my garment.'

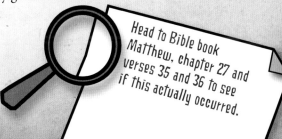

Head to Bible book Matthew, chapter 27 and verses 35 and 36 to see if this actually occurred.

41

DOZEN DAYS DECODED

As you will have discovered by reading this book, the Bible is packed full of info about Jesus, from beginning to end. But did you know that the popular carol *The Twelve Days of Christmas* also has loads of stuff in it about Jesus? Let me explain.

This popular Christmas song was written hundreds of years ago and, so the story goes, when Catholicism was outlawed in England (from the sixteenth through to the early eighteenth centuries), Catholics were not allowed to teach their children at home or in Catholic schools, but had to do things the way the Church of England at the time said.

According to tradition, *The Twelve Days of Christmas* were all the things that Catholic parents wanted to teach their kids (but written in a sort of code that only they were able to understand). Sneaky or what!

We haven't got space to squeeze in the whole song but let's have a quick look at a few highlights.

The twelve drummers drumming symbolised the twelve most important things they believed about God and the Church.

The ten lords a-leaping were the Ten Commandments.

Nine ladies dancing were the nine fruits of the Holy Spirit, such as joy, peace and patience.

The six geese a-laying stood for the six days of creation.

The five golden rings represented the first five books of the Old Testament.

The four calling birds were the four Gospels of Matthew, Mark, Luke, and John.

The two turtle doves were the Old and New Testaments

And the partridge in a pear tree represented Jesus.

42 RETURN TRIP

The birth of a baby always marks the beginning of something new. Until they pop out of their mummy's tummy, nobody has a clue what they'll be like or, for that matter, what they'll look like (except for maybe a not-very-clear ultrasound scan or two). Not so with Jesus. As I said earlier in this book, Jesus (God's Son) was around when the world was made. And then there were all those adverts (or prophecies) in the Bible, giving people a heads-up from God about Jesus.

So when Jesus rocked up at Christmas around 2,000 years ago, this was not the first that the world had heard of Him.

But when Jesus died thirty three-ish years later, this was not the *last* the world would hear of Him.

If you fast forward to the very last book of the Bible (it's called Revelation), we are told that Jesus will crop up again to make a return visit to earth. This time it won't be as a baby in a manger but as a conquering hero. Why's that? Easy. There's a lot of bad stuff that goes on in the world and a lot of this bad stuff is because of bad people. Those bad people take their lead from God's No. 1 enemy, Satan. Remember him?

The Bible tells us that there will be a day when Jesus calls time on His enemies and comes back to defeat them once and for all, which is good news for us.

WILD WEDDING

Unlike most parents, Jesus' mum and dad (Mary and Joseph) didn't have to worry about choosing a name for their baby boy. An angel of God had already told them He'd be called Jesus, so that made life a lot easier.

As you read the Bible, you'll soon discover that Jesus has loads of names or things He's called such as Alpha and Omega (meaning beginning and end), Immanuel (meaning God is with us) and Holy One of Israel (the land in which He was born).

Another, slightly unusual, thing the Bible calls Jesus is Bridegroom. This could seem a little odd because Jesus never got married so He'd have never have been a bridegroom.

So why does the Bible refer to Jesus like this?

It's all to do with the love Jesus has for His Church, which the Bible tells us is like the love a husband has for his wife (or should have).

Right now, Jesus' Church is down here on planet Earth and Jesus is up in heaven.

The Bible says that one day Jesus (the Bridegroom) and His Church (the bride) are going to get married and be together forever.

Unlike some weddings, there's no limit to the number of people who can attend. Everyone gets invited to the wedding if they make Jesus No. 1 in their life.

You can read about this wedding in Bible book Revelation, but just so you know, when it refers to Jesus it calls Him the Lamb.

Off you head to Bible book Revelation, chapter 19 and verses 6 to 9.

44
DIVINE DUNKING

lthough the first Christmas story is all about the birth of Jesus, another baby boy gets a big mention as well. It's none other than John the Baptist. In case you were wondering, he wasn't called that at the time. The 'Baptist' bit was added later, which I'll explain shortly.

John was related to Jesus and arrived on the scene around six months before him. This wasn't a coincidence. One day John was going to have a big part to play in Jesus' life. In the same way that John was born ahead of Jesus, when he grew up John would also once again go ahead of Him. What do I mean by that?

John had been singled out by God from birth to be the person who announced to the world that Jesus was the Son of God. An angel of God had told his dad (Zechariah) the sort of life John was going to lead.

First off, John wasn't to touch wine or strong drink.

Next up, John would be filled with God's Holy Spirit while he was still inside his mum, Elizabeth's tummy (or womb if you prefer to be technical).

And finally he would get the people of Israel ready for Jesus.

John did this by encouraging people to turn away from living lives without God and to get baptised to demonstrate that they'd done this.

John did that by dunking them in the River Jordan.

One day Jesus showed up and John was ready and waiting to shine the spotlight on Jesus.

YOU CAN'T BE TOO CAREFUL!

Read how he did this in Bible book John, chapter 1 and verses 29 to 34.

45
NATTY NATIVITY

When it comes to Christmas, most people seem to have their own family traditions. One of ours is getting the Christmas decorations down from the loft and hunting out our wooden nativity scene.

Once we've removed the tissue paper wrapping from each piece, it takes pride of place on our bookcase, with Jesus in the manger, centre stage.

We're not the only people who do this and nativity scenes aren't just to be found in homes. Shops and churches also have them.

Nativity scenes come in all shapes and sizes. Some just have Mary, Joseph, Jesus and a few animals. Others go for the whole works and include the wise men, the shepherds and even some angels thrown in for good measure.

So where and when did this Christmas tradition begin? Well obviously the idea started with Jesus being born and the Bible story that goes with it. But what about the nativity scenes and the figurines? How did they start?

As far as anyone knows, the credit for the natty nativity idea goes to a chap called Saint Francis of Assisi who, in 1223, set up the world's first real-life nativity (with live animals and real people) in a cave in Italy.

His reason for doing it was the same reason some people have nativity scenes today. He was fed up with people leaving Jesus out of Christmas. It's fine to give presents and to have a bit of a knees-up at Christmas, but let's not forget that it's Jesus' birth we're celebrating.

Within a hundred years, every church in Italy was expected to have a nativity scene and eventually the tradition spread right around the world.

If you're wondering why it's called the nativity, I'll tell you. It's because the word nativity means birth, which is what Christmas is really about. Jesus' birth. Now you know!

46

BIT PART JOSEPH

Although Jesus' dad, Joseph appears a few times in the Christmas story, it's his wife Mary who usually steals the limelight.

She gets chosen by God to give birth to Jesus while all Joseph gets to do most of the time is stand on the sidelines as a bit of an onlooker.

Of course we know that an angel visited Joseph to let him know about Jesus, and another angel gave him a heads-up to hot-foot it to Egypt (with Mary and Jesus) to escape from the evil clutches of horrid Herod.

But I think it's high time we bigged-up Joseph a bit more, so that's what I'm going to do.

Joseph might not have had a major part to play in the birth of Jesus (although he did take care of Mary when they travelled to Bethlehem) but there's every chance that young Jesus followed in His dad's footsteps and went into the family business.

According to the Bible, Joseph was a carpenter so it's quite possible that Jesus also became a carpenter.

Okay, so the word the Bible translates to give us the word 'carpenter' could also mean a craftsman but whatever it meant, if Jesus took after His human dad, He became skilled at working with His hands.

Wouldn't you have liked to have been a fly on the wall in their workshop, listening to their chit-chat? Although the Bible doesn't say anything about this, I'm convinced that Joseph must have been a really positive influence on His son, knowing that God had a special plan for Jesus' life.

It was precisely because of the ordinariness of Jesus' upbringing that later in life people questioned whether He was indeed the Son of God.

PERPLEXED PARENTS

Phew! It's quite hard work, finding a whole 50 Christmassy stories in the Bible. (I wonder if you can think of any I might have missed?) And this is because there's not a whole heap of information about Jesus' birth and childhood in the Bible.

To prove my point, the wise men, shepherds and angels don't even get a look in from the guys who wrote Bible books Mark and John. And once Matthew and Luke have said their bit about the Christmas story, they're ready to skip the next thirty or so years of Jesus' life as if nothing of importance happened to Him.

Well that's not completely true. Credit where credit's due. Luke does slip in a story about Jesus a year before He became a teenager. Want to hear it? Well let me spill the beans.

Every Jewish boy, when they reached the age of twelve, had to go through a religious ceremony that took them from being a child into being a man. It's called a Bar Mitzvah. You may have heard of it. Nowadays they do it at the age of thirteen.

In the Bible bit from Luke, we're told that Jesus' mum and dad were heading to Jerusalem with a large group of people for Jesus' Bar Mitzvah.

On their way back they travelled a whole day without realising that Jesus wasn't with the group.

Now that He was officially a man He didn't need to stick close to His parents every step of the way and they probably assumed He was somewhere in the big group travelling with them. Not so!

48
HEAVENLY HELPERS

Have you noticed that angels pop up quite a bit in the Christmas story? Well if you haven't allow me to remind you that angels showed up to tell Mary (Jesus' mum) that she was going to have God's Son, and then to tell Joseph (Jesus' human dad) about it.

Next up there's the angel who rocks up to inform Zechariah that he was also going to have a son who would one day tell people who Mary and Joseph's little boy really was.

And lastly, who can forget those shepherds who had a surprise night time visit from not just one angel but a whole sky-full, all of them giving thanks to God for the birth of Jesus.

So who exactly are angels and are they real?

They certainly are and the Bible mentions them plenty of times.

In fact, someone, with far too much time on their hands, has counted the number of times angels (or angelic beings) crop up in the Bible and they reckon it's around 270-ish. We'll take their word for it!

Angels work for God and spend their time going back and forth from heaven to earth delivering messages from God and looking after people.

Angels aren't like you and I, which means that they can appear and disappear at the drop of a hat. Sometimes they'll look like ordinary people and you might not even know that they're an angel. At other times they show up looking bright, shiny and larger than life.

49

A BRIGHT IDEA

Most people nowadays have heard of a Christingle (a decorated orange with a lit candle inside), but did you know that long before they'd been invented a guy from the Bible called Isaiah said something that would be the basis for this popular Christmas tradition?

Here's what he said: 'The people walking in darkness have seen a great light; on those living in the land of deep darkness a light has dawned.' You can find this in Bible book Isaiah, chapter 9 and verse 2. (I think it is so cool, having a book in the Bible named after you!)

Like so many Christmas traditions, Christingle came from Germany. The world's first Christingle service was in 1747 and once the children were all holding their lighted candles, the church minister said this prayer: 'Lord Jesus, kindle a flame in these children's hearts, that theirs like Thine become.'

If you've ever seen a Christingle you'll know that right in the middle of the orange there's a candle. It symbolises how Jesus brings light into dark places. Isaiah's words were a heads-up to the people who were going to be Jesus' neighbours that He was someone special sent from God.

The first Christingles didn't have an orange (to represent the world to which Jesus came) but just a candle wrapped with some red ribbon.

If you know anything about the Christmas story in the Bible, you'll know that red ribbon isn't mentioned anywhere. So why is it used? To get our answer we need to skip ahead in time to the Easter story. The red ribbon reminds us that one day the baby in a manger would shed His blood when He died for us on the Cross.

To find out if Jesus believed Isaiah's words, look up Bible book John, chapter 8 and verse 12.

50

HAPPY ENDING

Well, that's just about it for this book of Christmassy Bible stories. As we come to the end of our book I thought it might also be a good idea to see how the Bible ends.

At the very beginning of the Bible we're not only told that God made the world but that it was good.

I've mentioned it before but Jesus Himself was actively involved in the process. I've also mentioned that the world's first two people (Adam and Eve) made a bit of a mess of things and damaged our friendship with God, opening the door for all the bad stuff that now spoils the world. And finally, I've also mentioned that the reason Jesus visited this planet on that very first Christmas was to clean up this mess and to get things back to the way God intended when He first created everything.

From the time Jesus was an itty bitty baby in a manger, until the time that He hung on a cross (to take away all the bad stuff in our lives), He was focused on making it possible for you and me to be best buddies with God.

It's one thing for us to get made new by God but what about the world in which we live? It's also looking a bit worse for wear in some places and needs a bit of a makeover, don't you think?

Here's the good news! God has already thought of that.

One day, everyone who loves Jesus will get to live on a spanking new planet Earth.

Now that's what I call a happy ending!

Read about it for yourself in Bible book Revelation, chapter 21 and verses 1 to 4.

Get into God's Word.
Every day.

Join the Topz Gang as they explore the Bible through daily Bible readings, puzzles, cartoons and prayers!

Read a bit of the Bible every day, explore lots of stuff about you and God – and crack puzzles along the way!

Available as annual subscriptions or single issues, published every two months.

To purchase, go to **cwr.org.uk/shop**
or call **01252 784700** or visit a Christian bookshop.

Learn about life with lots of laughs

To see the full range and to purchase, visit **cwr.org.uk/shop**
or call **01252 784700** or visit a Christian bookshop.